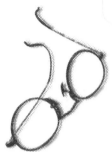

FORTY-SIXTY

A Study for Midlife Adults Who Want to Make a Difference

BY RICHARD H. GENTZLER, JR.

CRAIG KENNET MILLER

DISCIPLESHIP RESOURCES

P.O. BOX 340003 • NASHVILLE, TN 37203-0003
www.discipleshipresources.org

Reprinted 2002

Cover and book design by Nanci H. Lamar
Edited by Debra D. Smith and David Whitworth
ISBN 0-88177-325-5
Library of Congress Catalog Card No. 00-105308

DR325

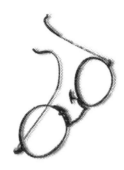

TABLE OF CONTENTS

Using This Book

Welcome to *Forty-Sixty: A Study for Midlife Adults Who Want to Make a Difference.* The purpose of this study is to help you understand the problems of midlife and to suggest ways of coping constructively with the most common dilemmas. Drawing on Scripture, it is a guidebook to aid the successful aging of midlife adults. Each chapter contains material related to midlife issues. Each chapter also includes a study guide that uses Bible study to enable the reader to draw upon God's word and wisdom for direction and meaning.

As you study *Forty-Sixty* by yourself or with others in a small-group setting, we hope you will realize that you are not alone in your journey. God, who made you, is also with you at every stage of life. Aging affords each of us an opportunity to grow in faith, in wisdom, in understanding, and in the ability to witness to others our faith in Jesus Christ regardless of the circumstances.

There are many books being written about the attributes necessary for successful aging, but it is important for each of us to find his or her own way. You can do this by listening to God, listening to your heart, and listening to your friends. There are no shortcuts and no easy answers. You are on an important, life-changing journey; may your travels lead you to a more fulfilling and more spirit-filled life.

USING FORTY-SIXTY AS A SMALL-GROUP STUDY

We encourage you to use this study with a group of people. We believe that learning is best done in groups. Although each individual faces his or her own midlife issues, sharing together can bring new insights to all. By studying together you will hear how others are coping with and are affected by issues and concerns of middle age. Understanding change takes time, but your time and energy investments in this group study will be profitable. At the end of the study, you will be better equipped for successful aging and for inventing new opportunities for ministry in your community.

Forty-Sixty can be used with existing groups such as Sunday school classes, weekday study groups, Bible-study groups, and so forth. It can also be used with a small group formed just for the purpose of doing the study.

STARTING A SMALL GROUP

Jesus' strategy was simple. He decided to invest his teaching and example in the lives of twelve people, his twelve disciples. This first, important small group in the New Testament established a pattern of learning and support that became fundamental to the life of the Christian church after the Resurrection.

According to Acts 2 the followers of Jesus gathered in homes for prayer, for teaching, for fellowship, and for the breaking of bread. This was the pattern of life for the early church. In eighteenth-century England, John Wesley followed the same pattern by organizing small groups called classes that met regularly to pray and to hold one another accountable to the gospel. A few years later, Philip William Otterbein was organizing Bible-study classes among the German-speaking people in America.

This pattern of ministry is very successful because it emphasizes two basic principles of discipleship:
• We learn best in groups.
• We grow in our faith when others encourage us and challenge us to grow.

Use *Forty-Sixty* to help you start small groups in your local congregation. It is equally valuable, however, for use among middle-aged adults who are neither church attendees nor members. The study is designed for a group of four to twelve people. If it grows beyond that number, participants should be encouraged to start a new group.

Forty-Sixty is designed so that over the course of ten sessions you will have the opportunity to meet regularly with a group, to grow in your relationship to God through Jesus Christ, and to become better equipped for successful aging.

Group Leadership

Forty-Sixty is designed to be led by clergy or laity or both. Leadership in the group may be designed in many different ways. We recommend that you share the responsibility for leadership. Consider a leadership team composed of the following members:

Leader (clergy or laity): Facilitates the sessions and helps participants work and learn together.

Apprentice Leader: Fills in when the leader is not available; is in training to lead another small group in the future.

Host: Takes care of the needs for hospitality by making sure the meeting space is comfortable and that people's needs are met. (Many times the group meets in the host's home.)

Apprentice Host: Assists the host; is in training to be the host for a future small group.

The primary goal for the leader of a small group is to enable the members to interact and dialogue with one another about the issues and topics in the sessions.

Leading the Sessions

At the beginning of each chapter you will find a session plan designed to help the leader guide the group through the session. Sessions are designed to be one hour in length, although some groups may want to schedule a longer period of time to allow for fellowship, refreshments, or more in-depth discussion. Some groups will find that a certain topic will be particularly relevant to their situation and will want to explore that topic in more depth after completing all of the sessions.

Each session follows a similar pattern. Components of the session include:

Getting Started

Each session begins with prayer. In the first few sessions the leader may pray. However, as participants get to know one another, the leader may ask others to pray.

In some groups the participants will have read the chapter to be discussed before the session. In other groups the participants will not read the material until they arrive at the session. Even if participants have read the material before the session, they will need a few minutes to review the chapter at the beginning of the session. In the "Getting Started" segment of the session, participants are invited to read or review the chapter and reflect on what were important points for them as they read. This helps everyone begin with a common frame of reference.

Discussion Starters

The discussion starters offer questions to help participants explore their own experiences in relationship to the topic of the chapter.

Biblical Reflections

During this segment the participants will be divided into smaller discussion groups of three to four to delve into a Bible passage that relates to the topic of the chapter. The book provides some short reflections and a few discussion questions to help the participants reflect on Scripture and their faith as they consider the issues and concerns raised by each chapter.

The goal of these sessions is not instruction. The goal is dialogue. Participants will undoubtedly learn more from one another than they will from reading the text. Breaking up into small groups allows more interaction to take place.

Making It Personal

In this segment the participants will focus on how they are personally dealing with the issues raised in the chapter. Often this will include some questions for the participant to answer and then discuss with the whole group or in smaller groups. The participants will begin to integrate into their own lives what they have learned from the text, from the Bible, and through dialogue with one another.

Closing

Each session closes with prayer and a reminder of any preparation needed for the next session.

What Are Some Useful Rules?

Some small groups start with a covenant to which everyone commits. The covenant guides the dialogue and interaction among group members. Some basic agreements are:

- Participants agree to give priority to meeting with the group for the ten lessons.
- Participants agree to read the chapter assignment prior to the small-group meeting.
- Everyone participates and no one dominates. All questions are encouraged; everyone's opinion is respected.
- What is said in the group stays in the group. Trust and confidentiality create an atmosphere for sharing and giving.
- The group is always open to new people who commit to the covenant.

1

Myths and Realities of Midlife and Aging

SESSION OUTLINE

Getting Started (10 minutes)
- Open with prayer.
- Ask participants to read or review Chapter 1.
- Ask participants to identify the key issues from the reading.

Discussion Starters (15 minutes)
- Use the discussion starters to help participants examine their own attitudes about aging.

Biblical Reflections (15 minutes)
- Ask for volunteers to read aloud Genesis 12:1-5 and 17:15-17.
- Divide into small groups of three to four if the group is large.
- Read the "Biblical Reflections" and discuss the questions.

Making It Personal (15 minutes)
- Read and discuss the "Making It Personal" section.

Closing (5 minutes)
- Ask participants to read Chapter 2, "Children, Parents, and Grandchildren," before your next meeting.
- Close with prayer.

Aging is one of those things that we tend to ignore until something happens to remind us that time is marching on. You realize that your birthday cake would look like a bonfire if you really put a candle in for each year of your real age. You see a nephew or a niece or the child of a friend and remark, "Look how big you are." Inwardly you realize that if they have changed, you must have grown older in some way. You catch a glimpse of yourself in a mirror and think, "Is that me?" All of these are natural signs of a change that is taking place as we move through time. How we approach aging makes a significant difference both in our quality of life and in the nature of our relationships.

Amazingly, some of the most important characters in the Bible made dramatic changes in their lives when they were older adults. Abram left his homeland to start a new people. His wife Sarah gave birth in old age to a son who would be the first of a new nation. Moses helped set his people free from captivity. These examples fly in the face of the idea that when you reach a certain age life loses its meaning and purpose. Instead each stage of life offers each of us new opportunities to respond to God's call.

When does middle age begin? At thirty-five? How about forty? Maybe fifty? For the purposes of this book, we will address the needs and concerns of people ranging in age from the forties through the sixties. We will use the term *Forty-Sixters* to describe this group. This term encompasses the whole generation of Baby Boomers (people born between 1946 and 1964) and it also includes a smaller percentage of people from the Silent Generation (born between 1928 and 1945). To a very real degree, these are the people at midlife. And since you are reading this book, you are likely to be a person in this age group, a person at midlife.

Our generation of midlife adults has altered every institution with which we have come in contact. We questioned authority, mistrusted institutions, listened to rock-and-roll, changed the workplace to a more casual style of work and dress, helped promote alternative medicine, and promoted the self-help movement. Many of us are dreamers and idealists, believing that we can and should have it all. As adults at midlife, we are busy. We are juggling children, parents, jobs, and spouses. We are saving and spending, although perhaps doing not enough of one and too much of the other. Many of us are parents of children who are under the age of eighteen. Also many of us have grandchildren, and because of the high number of single, working, and divorced parents, this generation of grandparents is much more involved with their grandchildren.

It's interesting how children can't wait to grow up. Ask a child of four how old she is and she'll quickly reveal her age, almost to the day, by saying, "I'm four and a half." Children look forward to getting older. They can hardly wait until they can get their driver's license or their first job during summer vacation. They look forward to graduating from high school and being "on their own." The future holds promise with the belief that someday they will be "all grown up."

However, once we hit that stage of life known as midlife or middle age, we find ourselves not quite anxious to grow older. In fact, few of us even think about our old age, except at our birthdays! Suddenly, time lived (counting from birth) becomes time left to live (counting toward death). Birthdays are sometimes put on hold, the thirty-ninth having become our society's "most celebrated."

Compare the birthday cards of children. A youngster's card proclaims in bright colors and bold print that another major milestone has been passed. It is a cause for celebration. There comes a point in everyone's life, however, when the message of the card turns to irony and sarcasm: "40 isn't old! Just ask anyone who's already reached that age!. . . But be sure to speak up and talk into their good ear. . . . Happy Birthday!" "50 is not the end of the world! . . . But you can see it from there. . . . Happy Birthday!" "So you're 60. Here's a Birthday Tip: Watch for these Five Warning Signs of Old Age: . . . 1. Memory Loss, 2. Uh, uh. . . . Happy Birthday!"

As a result of better healthcare, nutrition, job safety, medical technology, and physical fitness, people are living longer and healthier today than they ever have before. A person who is seventy today is more like a person at fifty was twenty years ago. Yet, we live in and are very much a part of an age-denying society. In America, if we're asked our age and we are sixty, we might say we're fifty-five. In some cultures, if persons are asked their age and they're sixty, they are more likely to say they're sixty-five. Greater respect is afforded to older persons in some cultures compared to the low esteem sometimes connected with older adults in our culture.

There are many reasons for this attitude. One is that our society places great emphasis on strength and beauty. When people have lost their strength and/or beauty, they are no longer valued. Another reason is the work ethic in our society. To have value, people must be productive, and if they are not productive, they have no worth, value, or purpose. So society deems unworthy those older people who have lost strength and beauty (at least by society's standards) and who are no longer commanding a salary. Therefore, persons at midlife may be fearful of getting older because they fear being considered useless!

Sometimes this attitude is gender-related. For example, Paul Newman and

Robert Redford, both over sixty, can command lead roles in movies and work with leading women half their ages. However, the reverse is seldom the case. Yet men are the ones who die younger than women. Furthermore, men who place all their self-worth in their jobs and then find their careers lacking or are nearing retirement may find it increasingly difficult to cope with the future.

Aging is God's good gift of life. Think of the alternative! However, as long as we cannot envision a graceful post-midlife period, people in their middle years will resist moving into this later life stage.

Forty-Sixters—once remembered for not trusting anyone over thirty—now caution society not to trust anyone under thirty (except maybe their own children and/or grandchildren!). And, although the middle years were once considered a static time, this generation of midlife adults is destined to redefine what middle age is all about.

Forty-Sixters are at the peak of their earning and spending power. But income and influence do not guarantee peace of mind or serenity. Most of us have some struggles in our forties, fifties, and sixties. Midlife has its special problems. In midlife we experience losses, changes, and fears. We look for something to hold on to or to grasp for support on our journey, but unless we have learned along the way, we may find our lives at this junction to be empty and unfulfilled. Dreams have been lost, misplaced, or abandoned. We set out to accomplish so much, and yet many of us wonder where the years went.

But there is hope. We can still grow. We can still dream dreams and see visions. At midlife we have a new opportunity. At middle age, we have a second chance. Midlife is a time for change, a time to give birth to our future and to enhance the quality of that future. We can deny the passing of time, the fact that we are actually getting older, but we can't deny the dreams. Dreams that have sometimes been lost, misplaced, or abandoned can be renewed, or new dreams can be formed. For the willing traveler, midlife affords an opportunity to reinvent, recreate, and renew.

Midlife is a time when we struggle with the "yearning of our hearts." A time when we begin to question the very foundation of our existence. It is a time when we set out on a new journey and begin to explore new pathways. As we travel on this road of middle age, the road leading to successful aging, we start wondering who we really are and why we are here. We begin to ask such questions as:

- What is life about?
- What am I missing in my life?
- Have I made the right choices in my life?
- What is it I really want and need to do?
- What excites me and gives me energy?
- How can I live so that my future is fun, rewarding, and useful?

Since we live in a culture that does not know how to age well, the Christian Church can and must serve a useful role in helping people of every age and stage to see and experience meaning and purpose in life. Throughout this book we will point to examples of people in the Bible who give us images of how to approach changes in life. Faith in God gives us opportunities to look anew at our lives and to ask, "What can I do today to make a difference for God?"

Recognizing the need to change and then following through with that change is not easy. One prerequisite to positive change is the willingness to face the truth about ourselves. It is important that we face our fears, our losses, our abandoned dreams in order for growth and renewal to begin. Developmental scholars call this a time of transition, a time of significant change in life patterns for better or worse. It is a time of great challenge and opportunity.

DISCUSSION STARTERS

1. Of the following products, which best describes your greatest fear about aging?

Depends	Viagra	Hair transplant	Hearing aid
Face-lift	Estrogen	Hair dye	Bifocals
Dentures	Fertility drugs	Memory drugs	Wheelchair

2. What are some of the changes that happen as people age? True or False:

_____ a. Life expectancy for women is seven years longer than for men.

_____ b. People sixty-five or older tend to view their health positively.

_____ c. The majority of people sixty-five or older no longer have sexual activity or desire.

_____ d. 23% of people over sixty-five live in nursing homes.

_____ e. As people grow older their ability to learn decreases.

(Check your responses against the answers at the bottom of the next page. What surprises you?)

3. What is your greatest concern about growing older?

BIBLICAL REFLECTIONS (GENESIS 12:1-5 AND 17:15-17)

God's call to Abram and Sarai came when Abram was seventy-five years old. They had no children, yet God promised that if they followed him not only would they have a child, but through their family line all the nations of the world would be blessed. As Abram left he gave up three things, his citizenship in his country, his status in the family clan, and his inheritance. Because of Abram's willingness to live a dramatically different life, a new nation was born. Years later God's promise that through his line all the nations would be blessed was fulfilled through the life and witness of Jesus Christ.

1. Why was Abram willing to give up everything to follow God?
2. Twenty-five years later, Abram was still waiting to see God's promise fulfilled. Why did he laugh at God?
3. Have you ever thought you were getting too old to try something new or that middle age was preventing you from living your life differently? What does this passage of Scripture say to such ideas? How does it speak to your life?

Making It Personal

Middle age can be a difficult stage of life when job and family responsibilities mount relentlessly. The years from forty through the sixties can be a time of frustration and even crisis for many people. Yet God still calls us to be faithful and obedient. But most of us are so caught up in the negatives of life, saying, "I'm too old" or "I don't have enough time" or "I've never done that before," that we let opportunities go by. If God never gives up, how can we give up on ourselves? Each day provides another opportunity to give to others, to make a difference for good in the world, to be a witness to the saving grace of Jesus Christ. The question we must each ask ourselves is "Am I listening?" For if we don't take the time to listen, how can we hear?

1. Do you agree or disagree with the statement above? Why?
2. What are some of the doubts or fears you experience in middle age?
3. In what ways would you like to make a difference for good?

ANSWERS for changes that happen as people age:
a. True; b. True; c. False; d. False; e. False.

Children, Parents, and Grandchildren

SESSION OUTLINE

Getting Started (10 minutes)
- Open with prayer.
- Ask participants to read or review Chapter 2.
- Ask participants to identify the key issues from the reading.

Discussion Starters (15 minutes)
- Use the discussion starters to help participants think about their current roles and relationships.

Biblical Reflections (15 minutes)
- Ask for volunteers to read aloud Luke 2:16-19 and 46-51.
- Divide into small groups of three to four if the group is large.
- Read the "Biblical Reflections" and discuss the questions.

Making It Personal (15 minutes)
- Read and discuss the "Making It Personal" section.

Closing (5 minutes)
- Ask participants to read Chapter 3, "Preretirement and Work," before your next meeting.
- Close with prayer.

The relationship of Mary, the mother of Jesus, and Elizabeth, the mother of John the Baptist, serves as an example we can relate to today. In Luke chapter one, we are given the story of two pregnancies, Mary's and Elizabeth's. Both were a surprise. Elizabeth was thought to be too old to have a child. In fact it took an angel to convince her husband, Zechariah, that she truly would. Mary, the virgin betrothed to Joseph, was still a teenager when an angel appeared to her and asked if she would be willing to give birth to the Son of God. Mary's reply was, "Here am I, the servant of the Lord; let it be with me according to your word" (Luke 1:38).

When Mary visited the much older Elizabeth they shared a common bond. They were pregnant with very special children. Rather than age, they were united by a life experience; each one was getting ready to have her first child.

In today's world it's not uncommon to find a lot of Elizabeths, women older than forty who are giving birth to children. Through the advance of health and biological technology, women are able to have children much later in life.

When attending a school program at an elementary school, it is increasingly hard to sort out who are the parents and who are the grandparents. Some parents in their fifties are sending their children to college while others are sending children to kindergarten.

In this atmosphere sometimes a forty-four-year-old new mother has more in common with a twenty-year-old new mother than with another forty-four-year-old woman who has no children or has five. While age and generations shape a person's values and beliefs, what an individual person is experiencing at the moment also has a great influence on the way he or she views the world.

People who are between the ages of forty and sixty-nine are not easily pegged as being at the same stage of life. While their age may be the same, their life experiences can be widely divergent. These differences are what makes figuring out the American family such a challenge.

While many would call us back to the traditional family of the 1950s, when Mom stayed at home with the children while Dad worked, the vast majority of American families are living in a complex web of relationships largely determined by the marriage pattern of the parents. Many people in their fifties have been divorced and remarried. Many also have children from previous marriages. On top of that they may be parents and grandparents of children under eighteen years of age at the same time. Throw in their relationship with their aging parents and they find themselves in the midst of a number of relationships that can be confusing.

Raised with the images of *Ozzie and Harriet* and *Leave it to Beaver,* many Forty-Sixters expected that family life would be a smooth progression from early marriage to retirement, with visits from the children and grandchildren. Instead, having a family is like living in a multiplex theatre. Each room of the house contains stories and experiences that are widely divergent, with family members dealing with everything from getting braces to using a walker, from changing diapers to preparing for the SATs. As one enters into the life experience of a fellow family member, one is not sure whether he or she is going to experience a drama, a suspense, or a comedy. It is hard not to be a critic or to try to write your own ending to the story.

Parenting and grandparenting bring unique challenges for Forty-Sixters that few are equipped for. As the culture has shifted over the last forty years, family life has been caught up in a whirlwind of changing values, expectations, and dreams. While parents navigate the changing lifestyles of their children, grandparents are asked to take on added responsibilities or are left out because of complications brought about by the marriage patterns of their children.

In the past the goal of parenthood was to raise children who would become mature, healthy adults. Today ask a room full of Forty-Sixters to define adulthood, and you'll get either blank stares or a list of characteristics that are not easily defined in real life. We used to say an adult was someone who was married, had at least one child, owned her or his home, and had a job that was self-supporting. Now we are more likely to say that an adult takes responsibility for himself or herself, knows who he or she is, can take care of himself or herself, or has other similar characteristics.

Returning to the account of Mary and Elizabeth, we see another image of parenthood. Mary and Elizabeth found themselves in unexpected circumstances in which they were called by God to raise two unique children. As they took the responsibility of parenthood, they did so with the expectation that they were not alone. They knew that in some way God was to play a role in the lives of their children. Their role was more than just making sure their children made it to adulthood; instead they found themselves in the midst of God's plan. Their purpose was not found in making their children successes, it was found instead in letting God's will be revealed as their children moved into adulthood.

As God's will was revealed, Mary and Elizabeth endured heartbreaking events; one of their sons was beheaded by King Herod and the other was put to death on a cross by the Romans. And yet through God's working in the lives of their children, the world was changed and God's mercy and grace were made available to all who believed.

Mary and Elizabeth challenge us to realize that parenting and grandparenting give us the opportunity to place our children and grandchildren in the stream of God's grace. Where that will take them, we trust to God. In the midst of the complexities of family life God gives us the strength, hope, and wisdom to shape the lives of those who are entrusted to us.

DISCUSSION STARTERS

1. What are your current life roles (parent, grandparent, spouse, sibling, friend, and so forth)?
2. How have your closest relationships changed in the last ten years?
3. How do you expect these relationships to change in the future?
4. What are your greatest concerns about your relationships?

BIBLICAL REFLECTIONS (LUKE 2:16-19, 46-51)

These two passages tell about the relationship of Jesus and his mother. While in many ways Mary's experience was truly unique, in other ways it reflects common situations between a parent and a child.

Many dramatic events led up to the birth of Jesus. When the angel Gabriel said that she was to be the mother of the Messiah, the Son of God, she replied, "Here am I, the servant of the Lord; let it be with me according to your word" (Luke 1:38). Nine months later, after arriving in Bethlehem, she gave birth to Jesus in a stable. Then shepherds arrived, telling her that they too had received a message from angels about her child. She must have had many emotions during this time—amazement, confusion, fear, wonder, and happiness, just to name a few.

Then when Jesus was twelve, Mary and Joseph took him with them to the Passover festival in Jerusalem. Rather than going home with his parents, Jesus stayed behind without telling them where he was. For three days his parents looked for him before they found him in the temple in Jerusalem.

1. How do you think Mary felt as she pondered on what she had experienced and had heard from the shepherds? What are the things that she may have particularly treasured and pondered in her heart?
2. What does the story of Jesus in the Temple reveal about Jesus' relationship with his parents? What does it reveal about Mary and Joseph's relationship with Jesus? What does it reveal about their relationship with God?

MAKING IT PERSONAL

Review the questions below with the following question in mind: How does the example of Jesus and his relationship to his mother help you see your personal issues from a different perspective?

1. How do you describe your own family situation?
2. For whose care or growth and development do you feel a certain level of responsibility? (child, grandchild, nephew, niece, sibling, parent, friend)
3. Who do you think feels responsible for you?
4. In what ways do you see God working in their lives? In your own?
5. What concern or issue most heavily weighs on you?

Preretirement and Work

SESSION OUTLINE

Getting Started (10 minutes)
- Open with prayer.
- Ask participants to read or review Chapter 3.
- Ask participants to identify the key issues from the reading.

Discussion Starters (15 minutes)
- Ask participants to answer the questions under "Discussion Starters."
- Invite participants to tell their answers to the first two questions. Explain that they will be dealing with the other questions later in the session.

Biblical Reflections (15 minutes)
- Ask for a volunteer to read aloud John 2:1-11.
- Divide into small groups of three to four if the group is large.
- Read the "Biblical Reflections" and discuss the questions.

Making It Personal (15 minutes)
- Read and discuss the "Making It Personal" section.

Closing (5 minutes)
- Ask participants to read Chapter 4, "Relationships," before your next meeting.
- Close with prayer.

When we meet new people, the first thing we usually do is find out their names and where they live. Next, we ask their occupations. In our society, work is central to identity, status, and economic well-being. "What you are" is often defined by "what you do."

Yet at midlife people begin to think about life beyond their working years. Because of downsizing and changes in the workplace, many Americans now quit work before reaching their sixty-fifth birthdays.

As midlife adults, work and career have defined much of our adult lives. While many of us are reaching our salary peak and are at the height of our professional prominence and work productivity, others of us are experiencing new problems and challenges with our work. Although many people still experience a linear pattern of work in one career, or at least in one field, throughout their lives, many others make two, three, or more career changes. Midlife is a time when we may consider career changes as we begin to reassess our lives.

Many of us at midlife continue to enjoy our work; but, for some of us, the thrill is gone. Stress in the work environment, gnawing job insecurity, and the realization of lost or unfulfilled dreams provide us with the impetus to feel dissatisfied with our work and careers. Many of us dream of a less-pressured lifestyle and find ourselves asking the following questions: Is this all there is to life? What am I doing in this job? Do I want to stay in this career? What is it I really want?

Jesus asked some of the same questions of himself as he was in his midlife years. In Jesus' time, life expectancy was much lower than it is today, so a person at the age of thirty would be in midlife. It was during this time that Jesus changed vocations; his role was no longer that of a carpenter but became that of the Messiah. It was at this stage of life that he fulfilled God's call in his life.

While his was one of the most radical changes of all time, we see colleagues and relatives who are changing jobs, discovering new talents and interests, selling their belongings, and moving to new locations and starting over. We begin to wonder if we shouldn't be doing the same thing. We may even begin to blame ourselves or our spouses, believing that if we (or they) had worked in another occupation and had made more money, we could take early retirement and live comfortably for the rest of our lives!

Some of us are just hoping to stay employed until we can retire. Although most people never think of it in such blatant terms, one thing many of us are looking for today is a job that offers secure employment regardless of economic climate or our own individual job performance. The reality, however, is that "job security" no longer exists. While our parents could work for the same company all their adult lives, we have little chance of doing that. Perhaps it is for this reason that many of us are retooling, building networks, changing jobs, exploring new interests, and moving to new locales.

Many women at midlife are reentering the full-time paid work force after years of raising children and working either in the home or at a part-time job elsewhere (which was usually done to help supplement the household income). This is a time of starting all over again. Upon reentering the work force, middle-aged women often find it necessary to change fields or jobs many times in order to be employed, find fulfillment, earn more money, or be promoted.

Some of us have no desire to stop working and find the idea of retirement unthinkable. This disposition may result from financial considerations or lifestyle decisions. If we are healthy, we may want to keep working but maybe not at our current job. Perhaps we have set our sights on a second career, or possibly a third or fourth. For us, keeping busy is critical to our own well-being. We like the satisfaction and meaning that work provides for our lives. Retiring is completely out of the question for us.

For others of us, we now have the seniority to call the shots and the technology to do the job at a remote site. We are finding new work patterns that provide us with more flexibility, more autonomy, an adequate income, an opportunity to be self-employed, and greater freedom to spend more time with our families. Work is suddenly more exciting, fun, and taking on a whole new meaning for our lives.

For others of us, however, retirement is something we look forward to and dream about at midlife. Unfortunately, retirement issues seem very distant when compared to the day-to-day pressures of work and family. It is not easy to focus on saving for retirement when faced with more immediate concerns such as job security, rising healthcare costs, putting the kids through college, and taking care of our aging parents. We keep putting off preparing for retirement until "sometime in the future." The worrisome part is that issues of financial planning and economic security for later years are no longer just future concerns. These issues are present-day imperatives. If we do not address these issues now, many of our futures will indeed be bleak.

Perhaps we have read newspaper articles and heard TV commentators suggesting that our generation is not doing enough to ensure long-term financial security. They suggest that we are not saving enough and that many of us will reach retirement with little or no savings. In reality, some of us may be "surprised" to discover how meager our resources really are.

Okay, so how much money do we need on the day we retire? Of course, there is no simple answer. It depends on many factors, including: how much income we can count on from a pension plan, Social Security, personal savings, and a possible post-retirement job (and whether it is full-time or part-time). It also depends on how wisely and aggressively we invested, the inflation rate between now and then, and how long we can reasonably expect to live. Whatever the amount, we'll probably need to save a lot more money than our parents did to be able to afford a comfortable retirement.

The fate of midlife individuals will vary, depending on how much we've saved and how well we've planned for retirement. Many midlife adults would like to retire early but are not saving enough for retirement. Many will need to work beyond sixty-five. As midlife adults are we planning to work into our seventies and eighties and reinvent ourselves every decade? How will we reconcile a dream of early retirement with our meager retirement savings?

One thing is clear, it is never too early to plan for retirement. Many of us can begin right now to create a better plan for our future. Unfortunately, for many of us the thought of retirement planning, trying to map out the next twenty or thirty or more years, is overwhelming. But like most of life's significant events, a secure and comfortable retirement doesn't just happen. It occurs through careful planning and thoughtful consideration about how you would like to live later in your life. Planning now can contribute to making your retirement years more secure—emotionally, physically, and financially.

Some of the things you can do to get started are:
- Reexamine your financial situation. Consult a qualified financial planner to help you in this important process.
- Find out where you stand with Social Security in terms of credited work units and projected benefits.
- Evaluate your pension plan. Consider participating in any matching plans your employer offers.
- Develop secondary job skills that could help you work later in life, if necessary.

Beyond the financial considerations are other questions that relate to core personal issues. After retirement will my life still have meaning and purpose? Will I be one who is dependent upon others, or will I have something to give back to others? Are the changes I am thinking of making simply for my own survival, or does God have something to say to me as I look at my own personal future? Where does God's call fit into my future lifestyle?

DISCUSSION STARTERS

1. How satisfying is your current work?

___ Very satisfying

___ It's not as good as it was when I first started.

__ It gets me a paycheck so I can do the things I like to do.

__ If I could I would do something else.

2. What is your attitude toward retirement?

___ I can hardly wait.

___ I will never retire.

___ I would retire now if I could afford it.

___ I'm afraid after retirement I will die on the vine.

3. What motivates you to get up in the morning?

4. Are you investing in relationships as well as in the bank?

5. What changes do you need to start thinking about today that will give you a better life in the future?

6. Where does God's call fit into your future lifestyle?

BIBLICAL REFLECTIONS (JOHN 2:1-11)

In this account we see Mary and Jesus as adults. Joseph has apparently passed away, and Jesus is now the head of the family. The opening phrase, "on the third day," is a direct link to the preceding verses that tell of Jesus' baptism by John the Baptist. When John saw Jesus, he proclaimed, "Here is the Lamb of God who takes away the sin of the world!" (John 1:29). At his baptism, Jesus confirmed God's call and began a new life. He went from being a carpenter to being an itinerant teacher and preacher. The next two days he called the first disciples to join him. Like Jesus, the disciples were embarking on a new way of life.

On the third day, Jesus and his new disciples attended a wedding where his mother was in attendance. Suddenly a crisis occurred. The wine was running out. All the residents of Cana were there, and no one would forget the wedding couple who did not provide enough refreshments for their guests. Mary asked Jesus to help. Jesus performed the first sign that showed him to be the Messiah: he transformed the water into wine, just as through his sacrifice and witness believers are transformed from sinners to saints.

In this story we see Jesus making the first public acknowledgement of a new lifestyle. His life would never be the same. From now on his relationships would be shaped by his new identity as one fully committed to what God was calling him to do.

1. What does this account say about Mary and Jesus' relationship?

2. What was Jesus' reaction to his mother's request?

3. How do others help you see the changes you need to make?

4. If you were truly to do what God was calling you to, how would that change what you are to become in the future?

Making It Personal

Review your answers to the questions in "Discussion Starters." How does the example of Jesus and his life change help you see your personal issues from a different perspective?

4

Relationships

SESSION OUTLINE

Getting Started (10 minutes)
- Open with prayer.
- Ask participants to read or review Chapter 4.
- Ask participants to identify the key issues from the reading.

Discussion Starters (15 minutes)
- Use the discussion starters to help participants think about how much time they spend on relationships and how that affects their lives.

Biblical Reflections (15 minutes)
- Ask for a volunteer to read aloud Luke 6:43-49.
- Divide into small groups of three to four if the group is large.
- Read the "Biblical Reflections" and discuss the questions.

Making It Personal (15 minutes)
- Read and discuss the "Making It Personal" section.

Closing (5 minutes)
- Ask participants to read Chapter 5, "Aging Parents," before your next meeting.
- Close with prayer.

Today Forty-Sixters find themselves at a crossroads when it comes to their relationships. At the same time as they look at making changes in work or careers, they are also caught in the natural change that comes with caring for growing children or aging parents. They wonder, "Who is going to be with me for the long haul?"

This is a dangerous question, for it forces a person to look at himself or herself and to ask what he or she is doing to invest in having deep, sustaining relationships with others. This self-appraisal happens whether a person knows it or not. Because the needs of a person change as he or she ages, what one desires from a relationship changes as well.

For many in this age group, marriage is the most significant relationship. At midlife marriage can be filled with new adventure and greater opportunity for love and intimacy. Despite delayed marriage and high divorce rates, middle-aged adults are most likely to be part of a married-couple family. But marriage during the middle years can also become commonplace. Family, jobs, and stress all have a powerful impact on marriage. If we have not been growing and forming an intimate relationship with a spouse throughout the years, by the time we reach midlife, the marriage may be lifeless.

In some cases, just when a man at midlife wants to establish a closer relationship with his wife, she has begun looking for greater autonomy and for interests outside the home and marriage. With her children becoming more independent or grown, a woman may seek new ways to explore meaning and purpose in life. Possibly, as women take on greater responsibilities and interests outside the family, and men become more interested in close relationships, their paths may cross.

The growing need of both partners in middle age to express individuality may threaten the marriage. If as a couple they fail to develop a new intimacy in midlife, they may find that they no longer have any common interests. They soon discover that while they have time together, they have nothing to share in that time. Couples in the middle years need to reassess and reaffirm individual goals and dreams as well as the future of the marriage relationship.

It is no surprise that many people in midlife go through a divorce. Or that many are ready to cast off their old friends to find people who bring more fulfillment to their lives. For many, underneath a longing for something new or different is a feeling of loneliness that drives them to seek a cure in any number of ways.

Whether it is drugs, alcohol, sex, entertainment, or food, the world offers many sedatives to those who are afraid to face their own needs for love and intimacy with another person who knows them as they are.

It is more perplexing that even when a person realizes this deeper need, her or his lifestyle at midlife seems to put so much in the way. Because of the demands we may put on others and on ourselves, few are the times when we actually have a conversation with each other.

A recent article in a national magazine said that the way to get ahead at work was to change jobs. Not just once, but about every two to three years. But while each time you may end up with better pay, what happens to the relationships you form with those with whom you work? If your goal is to figure out how to get to the next company, then you have little self-interest in developing friends at work.

In marriages with children, spouses may find that rather than focusing on the needs of one another they spend much of their time focusing on how to take care of the children. In two-career families the task of developing a deeper relationship with a spouse is even more of a challenge, because so little time is found to develop it.

People who are single may find it increasingly difficult to make friends in a culture that prizes movement and change. In a culture where busyness is the norm, where do people find the opportunities to invest in relationships? Whether someone is single by choice or by chance, lasting and growing relationships with others are important. We all have the need to love and to be loved, whether we are married or single. And we all want to be needed and respected.

As Jesus began his ministry he decided on a radical strategy. He decided to invest his time in the lives of twelve disciples. In Luke 6:12-13, 17-19, we find a pattern that shows us his primary relationships:

> Now during those days he went out to the mountain to pray; and he spent the night in prayer to God. And when day came, he called his disciples and chose twelve of them, whom he also named apostles. . . . He came down with them and stood on a level place, with a great crowd of his disciples and a great multitude of people from all Judea, Jerusalem, and the coast of Tyre and Sidon. They had come to hear him and to be healed of their diseases; and those who were troubled with unclean spirits were cured. And all in the crowd were trying to touch him, for power came out from him and healed all of them.

As Jesus embarked on his new career as the Messiah, he knew the demands on his life would be great. Rather than being the lone ranger who was going to save the world by himself, he made sure he had a support system in place that would sustain him during his ministry. His first focus was on his prayer life with God. If you read through the Gospels you find that key points of change in his life are preceded by deep times of prayer.

His second focus was on developing a smaller group of people who were his closest followers. Before facing the crowd, he put his relationship to God and to those closest to him in order.

This change was not without its problems. In Luke 8:19-21 we find this passage: "Then his mother and his brothers came to him, but they could not reach him because of the crowd. And he was told, 'Your mother and your brothers are standing outside, wanting to see you.' But he said to them, 'My mother and my brothers are those who hear the word of God and do it.' "

As Jesus entered his new lifestyle, his mother and brothers came to see him. They probably wondered what he was doing. While his words may sound like a rebuke of them, he was making a critical point with his disciples. Those who followed God and adopted this new way of living were his family. Jesus knew that without prayer and deep relationships his ability to carry out God's call would be severely limited. Before he went out to save the world, he focused on his relationships with God and with his closest friends.

Discussion Starters

1. How much time did you spend yesterday (put in minutes; does not have to add up to twenty-four hours, can overlap):

___ Sleeping

___ Attending to personal care

___ Eating

___ Exercising

___ Being entertained (TV, video, etc.)

___ With children/grandchildren

___ With spouse/significant other

___ In significant one-on-one conversation

___ Involved with sports or the arts

___ Praying/reading the Bible

___ Driving

___ Doing household chores

___ Working

___ Playing

___ Using the computer

___ Reading

___ Worshiping

___ Other

2. What surprises you about your list?
3. What was the best part of your day?
4. What was the worst part of your day?

Biblical Reflections (Luke 6:43-49)

Luke 6:20-49 is known as Jesus' "Sermon on the Plain." Much as he did in the "Sermon on the Mount" in Matthew, Jesus uses this opportunity to spell out to his disciples and the crowd what it means to follow him. As he concluded his thoughts he focused on the heart. Each person produces either good fruit or bad. What is seen on the outside comes from inside the heart. In the parable of the builder, Jesus gave the commonsense illustration of the difference between building a house on solid rock and building one on sand. Those who follow Jesus and act on his words build on a foundation that cannot be shaken.

1. Why is the foundation so important?
2. How are you building your foundation?
3. How does the nourishment of your heart strengthen your relationships?
4. How does investing in relationships help you stand the test of time?
5. How do your thoughts, words, and actions reflect your faith in God?

MAKING IT PERSONAL

Complete the following personal checklist with the following question in mind: How does following Jesus help you develop deeper relationships with those you love?

1. Which of the following keeps you from developing closer relationships?

_____ Demands at work

_____ The demands of raising children or grandchildren

_____ Lack of time

_____ A desire for something more, without knowing what that more is

_____ Lack of trust in others

_____ A question of whether I have anything to give

2. What would you be willing to give up so that you could spend more time developing deeper relationships?
3. How does your relationship with God help or hinder you in your relationships with others?

5

Aging Parents

SESSION OUTLINE

Getting Started (10 minutes)
• Open with prayer.
• Ask participants to read or review Chapter 5.
• Ask participants to identify the key issues from the reading.

Discussion Starters (15 minutes)
• Use the discussion starters to help participants think about issues related to aging parents or other relatives.

Biblical Reflections (15 minutes)
• Ask for a volunteer to read aloud Exodus 20:12.
• Divide into small groups of three to four if the group is large.
• Read the "Biblical Reflections" and discuss the questions.

Making It Personal (15 minutes)
• Ask participants to follow the directions in "Making It Personal."
• Invite participants to discuss insights they gained from the exercise.

Closing (5 minutes)
• Ask participants to read Chapter 6, "Losses," before your next meeting.
• Close with prayer.

W hen did you first look into the bathroom mirror and see, not yourself, but your mother or father staring back at you? For many of us, one of the first realizations that we are growing older is when we look into the mirror and see our parents. This experience can be pretty scary!

Adult children face two difficult tasks at midlife: (1) Finding appropriate ways of separating from parents to become psychologically autonomous (independent), and (2) giving responsible assistance to aging parents if they become frail.

Unfinished business from childhood may still challenge us. We find ourselves and our aging parents groping in the dark for ways of relating to one another. Over the years we have experienced unrealistic expectations concerning our parents. We internalized a set of rigid rules and inflexible roles placed on us by our parents. Achieving a relationship with our parents based upon understanding and acceptance as peers allows us to reach a level of maturity that will enhance our responsible choices if a parent becomes frail and needs assistance.

Seeing our parents age and become frail is not something we are fully prepared to handle. Over the years, we develop the fantasy of the omnipotent parent, someone who will always be there to give us guidance and advice whether we need it or not! Now, we begin to see our parents in a new and different light. We see them in all their humanness, including their frailties, weaknesses, and imperfections. It is at this point that we have a wonderful opportunity to develop a new relationship with our parents. A relationship built on true intimacy or at least a relationship free from parental intimidation.

With increased life expectancy, family members spend more time than ever before occupying intergenerational family roles. Many midlife adults have one, if not both, parents still living, and some have at least one living grandparent. Previous generations generally did not have the opportunity to interact with aging parents, let alone grandparents. Most adults did not live to reach old age. However, the lengthened life-span can lead to a greater likelihood that our generation of middle-aged adults will spend longer periods of time caring for disabled elderly relatives.

It is important to remember that not all older parents are alike. Most older adults maintain a high level of independence and health until the time of their death. The responsibility for their care may never need to rest with anyone but themselves. As adult children, we must work out a balance between independence and interdependence with our aging parents. Other older adults, however, may need a considerable amount of care.

Because older parents may resist adapting to changing circumstances, especially those involving increased dependency, we are faced with the decision about how and when to intervene in our parents' care. Assisting our aging parents can bring us and our parents closer together and enhance our relationship. Sometimes, however, caring for our aging parents can produce so much strain that it has negative consequences.

With increased life expectancy, we will likely spend more years caring for an aging parent than for a child. In addition, many of us may be rearing our young children or even our grandchildren and at the same time providing care for our aging parents. Caring for both our aging parents and our young children (or grand-children) produces a double burden in our lives. As a result, we face issues related to caregiving that are challenging, uncomfortable, and sometimes heartbreaking.

Spouses, too, are not immune to these conflicting demands, especially if they are women. The majority of caregivers are women: wives, daughters, and daughters-in-law. Generally, wives are the primary caregivers for their husbands and daughters are the primary caregivers for their mothers. This reflects both the greater longevity of women and their traditional role of personal care and nurture.

While we never undergo a complete role reversal, and we do not "parent our parents," changes in our role become evident. We may move from "advice-receiver" to "advice-giver." Eventually, we may be required to provide even more than advice. We may need to become completely involved in the primary caregiving of our parents.

However, we must remember that even though the parent is no longer able to care for himself or herself, we are not parenting our parents. Our parents will always be our parents, and we will always be their children. To think otherwise is to dehumanize and demean our parents. Even if one's mother reverts to childish ways or one's father babbles like a baby, that behavior does not make them little children. They are still adults and our parents.

As primary caregivers, we have to deal with a balance between parent care and our own lives, as well as our relationships with our spouses and children and our jobs. We are also likely to be dealing with both limited resources and inadequate knowledge concerning quality care. Caregiving may change our whole lifestyle, including: leisure time, privacy, social contact, physical well-being, and mental stability. We may also experience guilt, grief, anger, and emotional exhaustion from conflicting demands. However, recognizing and acknowledging the difficulties we experience should not minimize the feelings of love, care, familial bonds of affection, multigenerational appreciation, and responsibility that also accompany our situation.

If you are feeling physically and emotionally stressed from caregiving, here are some strategies:

- Set limits. Know how much time and effort you can give to caregiving, and then hold the line. If you need help, hire someone. If finances are a problem, press for more assistance from social services or other family members.
- Seek realistic solutions. Learn to live with less-than-perfect solutions. There are trade-offs related to caregiving; know when to use them.
- Ask for help. Contact healthcare providers, social-service agencies, and churches. If other family members aren't doing their share, let them know.
- Join a support group. Learn to share your experiences with others in similar circumstances.

For our aging parents, the later years are marked by losses. Some are physical—the loss of hearing and energy, for example—while others are emotional, such as the death of a spouse. Such losses are not only devastating but also chip away at a cherished self-image: that of an independent human being. Some older parents are determined to maintain control by hiding symptoms of failing health. For them, denial is a way of maintaining dignity and independence. For us, denial is an obstacle to evaluating our parents' situation.

It is important for us to be alert to changes in our parents' physical well-being or behavior. If a parent is not dressing properly or eating regularly, we may need to intervene. We need to watch for changes in weight, increasing falls, growing social isolation, and memory loss. Our goal is to ensure our parents' safety while respecting their individual autonomy. Honest communication, understanding, and empathy are vital for our well-being and for our relationships with our aging parents.

Discussion Starters

1. What advice would you give to your children (or other relatives) about how you hope they will relate to you as you age?
2. Based on your experience with aging parents or other relatives, what advice would you give to others who are dealing with aging parents?

Biblical Reflections (Exodus 20:12)

The first four of the ten commandments deal with our relationship to God. The next six deal with our relationships with others. The commandment to honor our fathers and mothers is the first of those that refer to human relationships. The fact that such a commandment is given indicates the age-old tensions that have existed between generations. Like the rest of the commandments, this one is addressed to adults. It reminds a younger generation of adults that they have responsibilities to the older generation.

1. How does a person honor his or her parents?
2. Why do you think the word *honor* is used in the command as opposed to *obey, protect,* or some other word?
3. How do you honor your parents?
4. How do you want to be honored by your children?

MAKING IT PERSONAL

Describe the nature of your relationship with your mother, father, and/or other older relative/friend. In your description answer some of these questions:

- Are you a primary caregiver?
- How are you helping another relative who is a primary caregiver?
- What fears or anxiety do you have about the future?
- Are you dealing with guilt or anxiety or anger about these relationships?
- What actions could you take to improve the situation?
- What help do you need as you work through these relationships?

Write in the space below, or on another piece of paper, how you will deal with these issues. Pray about your responses, and reflect on these issues during this week.

6

Losses

Getting Started (10 minutes)
- Open with prayer.
- Ask participants to read or review Chapter 6.
- Ask participants to identify the key issues from the reading.

Discussion Starters (15 minutes)
- Use the discussion starters to help participants think about the losses and changes they are experiencing and how they cope with them.

Biblical Reflections (15 minutes)
- Ask for volunteers to read aloud Psalm 71:9-22 and Acts 1:12-14.
- Divide into small groups of three to four if the group is large.
- Read the "Biblical Reflections" and discuss the questions.

Making It Personal (15 minutes)
- Ask participants to answer the questions in "Making It Personal."
- Invite participants to discuss insights they gained from the exercise.

Closing (5 minutes)
- Ask participants to read Chapter 7, "Lifelong Learning," before your next meeting.
- Close with prayer.

One of the most moving stories in the Bible is the one found in the Book of Ruth. Because of a famine in Israel, Naomi's family had moved to Moab. But while in Moab her husband and both her sons died. Despondent over her fate, she decided to return to Israel. As she was leaving she told her two daughters-in-law to stay with their own people where they could find other husbands:

> But Naomi said to her two daughters-in-law, "Go back each of you to your mother's house. May the LORD deal kindly with you, as you have dealt with the dead and with me. The LORD grant that you may find security, each of you in the house of your husband." Then she kissed them, and they wept aloud. They said to her, "No, we will return with you to your people." But Naomi said, "Turn back, my daughters, why will you go with me? Do I still have sons in my womb that they may become your husbands? Turn back, my daughters, go your way, for I am too old to have a husband. Even if I thought there was hope for me, even if I should have a husband tonight and bear sons, would you then wait until they were grown? Would you then refrain from marrying? No, my daughters, it has been far more bitter for me than for you, because the hand of the LORD has turned against me." Then they wept aloud again. Orpah kissed her mother-in-law, but Ruth clung to her. So she said, "See, your sister-in-law has gone back to her people and to her gods; return after your sister-in-law." But Ruth said, "Do not press me to leave you or to turn back from following you! Where you go, I will go; where you lodge, I will lodge; your people shall be my people, and your God my God. Where you die, I will die—there will I be buried. May the LORD do thus and so to me, and more as well, if even death parts me from you!" When Naomi saw that she was determined to go with her, she said no more to her. So the two of them went on until they came to Bethlehem. (Ruth 1:8-18)

Naomi and Ruth's conversation is so powerful because it reveals the deepest feelings of loss. Naomi thought her life was at an end. She saw no future ahead of her. On the other hand Ruth could not bear the loss of Naomi. No matter the consequences, she was determined to hang on to this precious relationship. Her statement "Your people shall be my people, and your God my God" rings out to us today. Through faith she hoped for something beyond the sense of loss she felt at that moment.

For many adults, midlife is a positive and enjoyable time of life. It is a period of transition, sometimes a jolting turning point, that prompts a change of perspective, feelings, and priorities. It is a natural transition from young adulthood to middle age.

But for others it is a time of facing loss. Forty-Sixters experience a sense of loss on many different levels. While this generation of midlife adults has rejected many of the images of middle age held in the past by their parents, it is important for us to recognize that we also have losses we're not used to experiencing.

While the inner quest at midlife usually results in more personal control, certainty, freedom, and financial security, we may also recognize a sense of loss and failure that life hasn't turned out the way we had hoped it would. We may experience the reality of lost friendships, the death of one or both parents, diminished faith, lessened stamina for things physical (including sex), faltering health, children who turned out to be "different" than we had expected, fewer opportunities for advancement, and the failure of the world to improve. Is it any wonder that at midlife many of us begin to go to bed earlier at night?

In midlife, many people experience their first serious illness as the prevalence of chronic illness rises. Arthritis, high blood pressure, hearing problems, and heart disease are among the most common ailments. As chronic conditions emerge, people spend more on healthcare products and services. Many middle-aged adults are joining health clubs to help keep physically fit and are seeing the inside of locker rooms for the first time since high school!

During midlife, relationships can change as much as our bodies. It is not a surprise that at midlife many couples become separated or go through a divorce. As children age and enter their young adult years, parents find their relationships with children shifting. Some may experience the empty-nest syndrome when their children leave the home. Relationships at work may shift as one takes on added responsibility or finds himself or herself downsized and looking for another place to work.

Some middle-aged adults experience a midlife crisis. The midlife crisis may have biological, emotional, vocational, and spiritual aspects. For women, this is likely to be a biological event which centers around menopause. With menopause, women end childbearing, but many go on with child-rearing and often grandchild-rearing, moving also to parent-caring and husband-caring—or perhaps to a new career or to college.

For men, the midlife crisis is often more of an emotional phenomenon involving self-image than a biological change. This crisis usually involves the job-related questions of self-esteem and fading dreams of ambition and financial success. For some men, the "answer" may be to rush out and buy a sports car or have an affair.

The death of a parent is one of the traumatic events many people experience during midlife. The death of a parent awakens people to their own mortality. It can also mean added responsibilities at a time of emotional distress. Caring for a surviving parent, administering the execution of a will, and disposing of property can all be time-consuming endeavors for middle-aged adults. This can be especially demanding if you live a great distance from your parent's home.

The death of a spouse may also occur during midlife, plunging the surviving spouse into a whirlwind of grief and anxiety. Coming to grips with the realization that the person you expected to grow old with is now suddenly absent creates a deep well of emptiness and a numbness for living. Taking on added responsibility for family, home, and job may make you cynical, angry, and depressed.

Others may experience a divorce during midlife. Even if the relationship was not a healthy one, nearly all people will still experience feelings of grief and loss.

The important point is that all change, regardless of whether it is perceived as helpful or not, is accompanied by some loss. Finding one's way in midlife demands that we confront our losses realistically. It requires that we face "the good, the bad, and the ugly" in our lives. It is a good time to evaluate how far we have come, appreciate what we have, acquire greater self-knowledge, and reassess our choices. Ultimately, managing midlife depends more upon motivational than on physical issues. It requires that we move through and beyond our grief. Are you cynical about your future? Bored? Feeling hopeless? Or are you eager to make your middle years the best years of your life? The answer to these questions determines your future—to live on or to decline.

DISCUSSION STARTERS

1. What movie or book title best describes some of your most recent disasters?

2. How do you handle loss?

_____ I hold it in

_____ I have to share it with someone else

_____ I pray

_____ I deny something has changed

_____ Other

BIBLICAL REFLECTIONS (PSALM 71:9-22; ACTS 1:12-14)

The words of Psalm 71 reflect someone who is facing difficulties and who perceives that aging is a disadvantage in dealing with these difficulties. The Psalmist speaks of enemies who seek to "pursue and seize" him, and he prays for God's help to sustain him in the midst of troubles.

The last time that we see Mary, the mother of Jesus, in the Bible is in Acts 1:14 after the death, resurrection, and ascension of Jesus. We find her with the disciples devoting herself to prayer.

1. What are the "enemies" that you feel are "pursuing" you as you age?
2. What hints does Acts 1:12-14 give us about how Mary coped with the loss of Jesus?
3. What guidance do these two Scriptures provide for us as we deal with loss?

MAKING IT PERSONAL

1. Which have you experienced?

_____ Midlife crisis	_____ Midlife career retirement
_____ Loss of mobility	_____ Need for eyeglasses
_____ Loss of hearing	_____ Need for false teeth
_____ Lack of energy	_____ Loss of your hair
_____ Divorce or separation	_____ Death of a significant loved one
_____ Loss of an hourglass figure	_____ Menopause
_____ Loss of physical strength	_____ Serious illness
_____ Breakdown of a close relationship	_____ Loss of job

2. How do these affect you today in your day-to-day living?
3. In what ways does your faith give you strength or hope in the face of loss?

7

Lifelong Learning

SESSION OUTLINE

Getting Started (10 minutes)
- Open with prayer.
- Ask participants to read or review Chapter 7.
- Ask participants to identify the key issues from the reading.

Discussion Starters (15 minutes)
- Use the discussion starters to help participants think about how they are currently learning.

Biblical Reflections (15 minutes)
- Ask for volunteers to read aloud Acts 19:11-20 and Ephesians 4:7-24.
- Divide into small groups of three to four if the group is large.
- Read the "Biblical Reflections" and discuss the questions.

Making It Personal (15 minutes)
- Ask participants to use the questions in "Making It Personal" to help them begin to develop a lifelong learning plan.
- Invite participants to discuss insights they gained from the exercise.

Closing (5 minutes)
- Ask participants to read Chapter 8, "Spirituality," before your next meeting.
- Close with prayer.

D o you remember sitting at your desk at school when you were a child? You may remember feeling bored. You were probably thinking that the day would never end. You were sitting there waiting for the final bell to ring to signal your freedom for the day. This is the way many of us felt through a good part of our school years.

We used to think that there were three major components of a person's life. The early years were singled out for learning, the middle years for working, and the later years for leisure (retirement). The first stage was acquiring an education. This included our schooling years of childhood, adolescence, and perhaps the early years of young adulthood. We knew we had to go to school, but we also knew (or so we thought!) it would not last forever. The schooling years were to provide us with enough information to help us move into, and sustain us throughout, our second stage of life: our working years. With our schooling years completed, we knew we would work for about forty years and then move into the third and final stage of life: our leisure or retirement years.

Back then, many educators believed that teachers simply poured education into people. Students were filled with many facts and with as much information as possible. As a result, people would turn out to be good and productive citizens and would know how to make use of their knowledge for the rest of their lives. This was fine when knowledge and technology changed very little over a long period of time. However, in an era of rapid change, information explosion, and technological revolution, this purpose of education is no longer appropriate.

Life seemed so much simpler then, didn't it? Today, in our complex and ever-changing world, our thinking about education is ever evolving and ever changing. Many of us were educated at a time when a high school diploma or college degree was believed to be terminal. Once graduated, we felt we were prepared for the rest of our lives. Experience has taught us that this is not true. We know that our learning during the so-called schooling years is not adequate for meeting the demands we face in our daily lives and in our workplaces today. The information we learned in school is outdated and ill serves us for facing the challenges in our world.

The explosion of information is changing who we are as middle-aged adults. We are far different people at midlife than those who were middle-aged fifty years ago. At that time, most people who worked in business and industry, farming, or many other occupations were not greatly concerned with continuing education. For the most part, people were able to succeed in life from experience and by using knowledge gained from the "schooling years."

Today, we are engaged in lifelong learning. We do not go to school and then move into the work world, never having to learn anything new ever again! We know that in our world of accelerating change, learning must be continuous and ongoing. We find continuing education providing us with the updating of skills to stay abreast in our current occupation or preparing us for another career.

If the concept of lifelong learning is an organizing and guiding principle for our lives, we will be better prepared to adapt to changes and to adopt new roles for meeting the challenges we face in our world. While the "schooling years" of our children are concerned primarily with developing the skills of inquiry, our education as middle-aged adults must be primarily concerned with using the resources and skills gained as self-directed inquirers. We learn new ideas and information not only in the formal settings of the classroom but in informal ways, such as in the workplace, on the Internet, and through media technology.

Unfortunately, education is not yet completely understood or assimilated in our society as a lifelong process. We are given few skills helping us to be better able to develop skills of inquiry. Workplace training departments, learning/education corporations, community colleges and universities, and church adult-education programs are not always effective in helping us, as middle-aged adults, develop the attitude that learning is a lifelong process. Nor are they always effective in helping us acquire the skills necessary for self-directed learning.

Today, knowledge gained at any point in time is largely obsolete within a matter of years and perhaps even months or less. Over the years, the pace will only increase, because the forces that are driving this change are so powerful. As midlife adults we must learn to think differently. The most important learning for us is learning how to learn, in other words, developing the skills of self-directed inquiry.

At one time, formal and informal learning in midlife was learning for its own sake. It was learning that related to one's own interests, inner life, or intellectual growth rather than learning that was meant to be used for professional or employment-related objectives. This is no longer the case.

While it is true that at midlife we want to make sense of and find meaning in our diverse life experiences, we are also constantly being challenged with new experiences and learning.

Learning is a permanent part of our lives if we plan to keep working or stay employed. In order to stay current, most people will need to relearn their business every three to five years. Our midlife years can be greatly enriched as we accept for ourselves the reality and the necessity of our continued learning and growing.

But learning for learning's sake is not the goal. Unless you are planning to go on a game show to answer trivia questions so you can win a million dollars, knowing stuff is not enough. A person learns so he or she can serve. What we do with our knowledge is as important as what we learn. Even John Wesley, the founder of the Methodist movement in England in the eighteenth century, published a collection of folk remedies for various illnesses and diseases called the *Primitive Physick*. His purpose was to put the best medical knowledge of the time into the hands of the people in the street.

As the computer and the Internet provide us with a world of information, the smart people are the ones who will learn to discern what brings meaning and purpose to one's life. As we struggle to keep up, those who can filter knowledge through the sieve of experience and faith will be able to determine what is true, healthy, and wise.

DISCUSSION STARTERS

1. From the following, identify your top three sources of knowledge:

___ Evening news	___ Internet	___ School
___ Work	___ Family	___ Church
___ Bible	___ Computer	___ Nonfiction books
___ CDs	___ Bible classes	___ Magazines
___ Television	___ Movies	___ Radio
___ Continuing education	___ Friends	___ Novels

How has this changed over the years?

BIBLICAL REFLECTIONS (ACTS 19:11-20; EPHESIANS 4:7-24)

The city of Ephesus was known for its knowledge of magical arts and sciences. Acts 19:18-20 tells how a group of Christian converts burned their magic books as a way to witness to their new faith in Jesus Christ. In contrast to the magical arts, Paul talks about the gifts of the spirit that equip people for ministry.

1. How are you to use your knowledge?
2. What is the purpose of equipping people for ministry?
3. What does it mean to be mature in faith?
4. What does it mean to live in the futility of our minds?
5. How do you renew the spirit of your mind?
6. How do these Scripture passages help you focus on what you need to learn?

MAKING IT PERSONAL

Develop a lifelong learning plan for yourself. Use the following questions to guide you as you develop the plan.

1. What are your goals for learning in the following areas:
    a. Work
    b. Relationships
    c. Spirituality
    d. Hobbies/Leisure pursuits
    e. Personal growth

2. In which area do I have the most strength?
3. In which area do I need the most growth and development?
4. Which area, if ignored, poses the greatest danger in the future?

8

Spirituality

SESSION OUTLINE

Getting Started (10 minutes)
- Open with prayer.
- Ask participants to read or review Chapter 8.
- Ask participants to identify the key issues from the reading.

Discussion Starters (15 minutes)
- Use the discussion starters to help participants think about their own spiritual lives.

Biblical Reflections (15 minutes)
- Ask for a volunteer to read aloud John 3:1-17.
- Divide into small groups of three to four if the group is large.
- Read the "Biblical Reflections" and discuss the questions.

Making It Personal (15 minutes)
- Ask participants to complete the Spiritual Journey Graph.
- Divide the group into pairs and ask each pair to use the questions in "Making It Personal" to reflect on their graphs.

Closing (5 minutes)
- Ask participants to read Chapter 9, "Death and Afterlife," before your next meeting.
- Close with prayer.

Herman, who is in midlife, was raised in an Amish community. He married an Amish woman and they raised their many children in the Amish faith tradition. Herman was a builder and a farmer. He lived out of the traditions of the Amish way of life.

Recently Herman underwent a drastic change in his life. He got rid of his beard, and in place of his black clothing and hat, he wore sneakers, jeans, a brightly colored shirt, and a baseball cap. Instead of a horse and buggy, Herman started driving a pickup truck. He was on a spiritual quest, one that was not without a high price to pay. Because of his questioning and seeking, his faith community, his bishop, his family—including his wife and children—and all of his Amish neighbors have "shunned" him (meaning that he is an outcast from the community and no one can have anything to do with him). Where Herman's journey will lead him, he does not know, but he is on a spiritual quest. Herman is a man searching for meaning in life. He is both fearful and hopeful in his quest.

When we reach midlife and the goals of young adulthood have been completed, changed, or found lacking, we often begin an inward journey seeking to know and nourish the self. Some may call this a spiritual crisis, but it is not a crisis in the usual sense. A spiritual crisis is understood as the creative movement that provides us with the opportunity to move on and to grow. Most of us will not go through a crisis like Herman's. But most will experience some type of spiritual crisis during our middle-age years.

Because we encounter spirituality differently at various ages and stages of our lives, the midlife transition is a turning point that opens the door to meaning and purpose for our lives. For some of us, when the children are grown and on their own, the empty-nest stage awakens a spiritual crisis within. For others at middle age, a spiritual crisis may develop upon the death of one's parents, a job loss, entering retirement, or the end of a marriage. It may be the realization that one's dreams will be unfulfilled. For Herman, the man in the story above, the crisis came when new members moved into his faith community and brought with them changes he could not accept.

We may have barely answered the question as a young adult, saying, "This is who I am," when we are toppled from this place of certainty by a midlife crisis. As a result, we find it necessary to begin all over again by asking in myriad ways, "Who am I really?"

Spirituality, if it is meaningful, must relate to our everyday experiences and give expression to our deepest feelings and concerns. It must provide us with the assurance that our own lives have meaning and purpose and are related to and part of something greater than ourselves. The renewed search for meaning in our lives over against the demands of job, family, and health concerns is an important and vital transition for our stage in life.

Most of us do not give much thought to spirituality. Sometimes we equate this with organized religion and the church institution. Spirituality and organized religion are not one and the same. Yet, many of us find the rites, ritual, liturgy, and music that is often part of organized religion and the church institution to be important in our spiritual journey.

Some of us equate organized religion and the church institution with rules that lock us into a set belief. We may believe that the church establishes barriers that hinder personal growth, require everyone to "march to the same beat of the drum," and keep everyone on a "personal guilt trip."

Others of us see spirituality as more open, with room for individual interpretation that encompasses our relationship to God, self, family, humanity, and nature. It is a shift away from organized religion to an individuality of faith. It is believing that our relationship with God is okay with or without religious organizations.

Many of us, however, desire to find a sense of community in our lives. While organized religion or the church institution may not be to our liking, the individual church or faith community is. We find in the local church our sense of belonging and place for community. It is here where our children and grandchildren receive religious education, where we experience mystery, fellowship, and worship. It is in the faith community that we are challenged, blessed, renewed, and transformed. It is here where we encounter God and experience God in relationship to self, others, and the world.

In the wider culture, we see through the media a renewed emphasis on the belief in prayer, angels, the supernatural, and the afterlife. This reflects a shift from a youth-oriented to an adult-oriented culture. With increased life expectancy and growing numbers of adults in midlife and older adulthood, our society is experiencing a transition from being youth-driven to being adult-centered. We are seeking the meaning of spirituality in our lives, whether we verbalize this idea or not. As a result, society, and in particular the media, mirrors and creates images that represent our yearnings, searching, and experiences.

After all, our generation of midlife adults has done much to contribute to the rise in religious feelings. We are the ones, after all, who attend the Promise Keepers rallies and make up the Christian Right. We are also the generation that has promoted the New Age movement and whose members have become adherents of Eastern mysticism. While we believe our religion is personally important, we think the influence of religion in America is declining. And yet, we are aware that more studies are linking health and religion. Some research shows that a positive correlation exists in people between practicing faith through prayer, meditation, Bible reading, or worship participation and good health.

As we reevaluate past values, beliefs, and lifestyles and consider future changes, we are seeking renewal for our lives. Knowing that we have experienced failure, disappointment, or disillusionment in our lives, we now seek sources and the means to become a transformed and renewed people.

Some people speak of a load being lifted from them by the awareness of God's presence and companionship. Others describe spiritual renewal in terms of the heightening of their natural abilities to think wisely and to act responsibly. Jesus refers to the midlife transition as spiritual rebirth. As Christian adults, we seek God's Spirit dwelling in us and giving us guidance and direction. This is most clearly evidenced in Scripture and through tradition, but it is also realized through reason and experience.

For many of us, midlife transition changes our direction. It is a shift in our thinking away from self to God. Because our earlier years have been spent in pursuit of success, materialism, and acquisitions, God's presence nearby may not be felt as clearly anymore. As we sense the losses and failures in life typical of midlife experiences, we want our lives to be different in the future.

Perhaps the bottom line in our midlife spiritual journey is the desire for confidence that we are good people, that our lives do matter, and that our existence makes a difference. We find it important to let go of the "me generation" and to find self-worth through selflessness. That is why many of us find Jesus so captivating. We see in Jesus one who epitomized selflessness and emptied himself completely for us.

Perhaps discovering for ourselves anew God's vision for our lives will lead us to spiritual maturity. One thing is clear: regaining a spirituality that allows us to see our own personal lives as moving toward wholeness, as filled with meaning, and as related to God, humanity, and all of creation is important for each of us in our middle-age years.

DISCUSSION STARTERS

1. Where do you find yourself closest to God?
2. What keeps you from drawing closer to God?
3. What promotes growth in your spiritual journey?

BIBLICAL REFLECTIONS (JOHN 3:1-17)

John's Gospel places Jesus in Jerusalem at the beginning of his ministry. During the time of the passover, a Pharisee by the name of Nicodemus visited him at night. We can surmise that as a leader of the Jews he did not want to be seen. Because of Jesus' miraculous signs, Nicodemus recognized that he came from God.

1. What was Nicodemus looking for?
2. How did Jesus respond to Nicodemus' spiritual crisis?
3. What did Jesus mean by saying a person must be born from above?
4. In what way do you identify with Nicodemus?
5. What did Jesus say was his own purpose in life?
6. When does eternal life begin?

MAKING IT PERSONAL

Think of your own spiritual journey. In the space below make a graph that shows the highest and lowest moments in your spiritual journey. On the graph use a key word or phrase to help you reflect on your spiritual journey.

Spiritual Journey Graph

High				
Low				

Birth   Childhood   Adolescence   Young Adulthood   Midlife

Reflect on these questions as you look at your graph:
1. What settings (places, locations, atmosphere) influenced your journey?
2. What was happening with your personal relationships?
3. In what ways did you grow spiritually as a result of your experiences?
4. What role (if any) has the community of faith played in this journey?
5. What spiritual disciplines (prayer, fasting, worship) have contributed to growth in your relationship to God?

9

Death and Afterlife

SESSION OUTLINE

Getting Started (10 minutes)
• Open with prayer.
• Ask participants to read or review Chapter 9.
• Ask participants to identify the key issues from the reading.

Discussion Starters (15 minutes)
• Use the discussion starters to help participants think about their own beliefs about death and afterlife.

Biblical Reflections (15 minutes)
• Ask for volunteers to read aloud Acts 7:54-60 and Revelation 7:15-17.
• Divide into small groups of three to four if the group is large.
• Read the "Biblical Reflections" and discuss the questions.

Making It Personal (15 minutes)
• Ask participants to answer the questions in "Making It Personal" and then to discuss their answers with one or two other people.

Closing (5 minutes)
• Ask participants to read Chapter 10, "Giving Back," before your next meeting.
• Close with prayer.

Our society has a fascination with death. Movies about ghosts, angels, and near-death experiences are popular viewing. Perhaps this is because death is so removed from us in our living. Modern advances in science have lengthened life expectancy, while our contacts with death are fewer and farther between within our families.

Most of us no longer live in rural settings that subtly but constantly remind us of the natural cycles of birth and death: planting and harvesting and the slaughtering of animals for food. At one time the whole family was exposed to death: children often witnessed the dying and death of grandparents. In many cases, children helped care for their dying grandparents. Today, however, death usually takes place outside the home, often in a hospital or nursing home. Even if the dying person is in the home, many family members are not present. Children and grandchildren may live many miles away and only return at the time of the funeral.

By not being exposed to death, we have become a death-denying society. We believe that death just won't happen to us. We even try to live as if death will never come our way. Despite its prevalence in popular entertainment, death is, paradoxically, a taboo subject, something we don't talk about. There is a superstitious belief that if we can avoid seeing or speaking about death, it won't happen. We feel, perhaps only subconsciously, that to be in contact with death in any way, even indirectly, somehow confronts us with the prospect of our own deaths and draws our own deaths closer.

Many people simply do not say *dead*, *death*, or *die* but speak of death metaphorically or euphemistically. We compare death or dying with more pleasant things in our experience, things with which we are familiar. We compare death to being asleep, passing on, passing away, expiring, going home, being lost. The four-letter word *DEAD* is almost pornographic. Some of us even refuse to prepare a will (even a "living will") or to discuss plans for our funeral and burial, believing that such talk is morbid or will actually hasten our own demise!

We have come to believe that death may be postponed for a significant duration. After all, life expectancy in the United States has greatly increased during the last century. This has occurred through disease control, improved sanitation, better public health, affordable healthcare, more knowledge of and adherence to good health practices, modern medical advances, better nutrition, improved job safety, lower infant mortality, and a host of other developments. As we become more informed and more willing to pursue healthful lifestyles (giving up smoking, participating in physical fitness and exercise, forming better nutritional habits, and so forth) and as there are more and more medical advances, life expectancy is likely to continue to increase.

In addition, our growing technological control over our world has led us to feel uncomfortable about anything that we cannot control. Death appears as a contradiction to our self-appointed role as the masters of our destiny, and so we do our best to deny death.

Yet, all of us at some time or another will confront the inevitability of death—our own death. The realization of our own death may become heightened during our midlife years. We begin to see and to hear about the death of former classmates and colleagues. We experience the death of loved ones and family members. At midlife, many of us will experience the death of at least one parent. With the death of a parent, we come face-to-face with the realization of our own mortality. Prior to midlife, we measured time from birth; now at this stage of life, we begin to measure time till death.

As middle-aged adults, we may resist the reality of aging as life begins to look much too short. Since our horizons must now hold the possibility of our own death and the death of those nearest to us, it is important for us to come to an understanding of life that includes death. Every living thing will eventually die.

Although we are confronted by the reality of death, at midlife it is not usually our own death; rather, it is the death of someone we love. Some of us may experience the death of a spouse or of children. However, for most of us, death becomes a reality because we face the death of our parents. For the first time in our lives, many of us will experience the pain and grief related to death as a direct result of the death of someone we love.

Confronted by grief, we experience feelings of sorrow, anger, guilt, fear, and confusion. The extent and duration of grief vary from person to person, often depending upon the closeness of the relationship and/or the preventability of the death. We know that death is not reversible and that life goes on without the deceased; however, the challenge of coming to a point of acceptance is not easy. Grief is painful, but it is also necessary.

Grief is a natural part of the human experience. Faith plays a major role in grief of any kind, but not in the way some people think. Some people seem to have the idea that a person with strong faith does not grieve and is above this sort of thing. To say a person is deeply religious and therefore doesn't experience grief or pain is ridiculous. Grief, like birth and death, is an essential part of the human experience. It is not always easy to "let go" and to "move on." We mourn the death of someone we love because we feel the pain of loneliness and sorrow. As we move through the process of grief and bereavement, we are able to disengage or detach from the deceased loved one for the purpose of reattaching or reinvesting fully in life.

The death of others always leaves a gap in our own lives. Mourning because of loss is a natural and human reaction. Yet it may also be the opportunity for living with renewed strength. We must experience the loss fully (intellectually, emotionally, physically, and spiritually) in order to be available to reinvest fully in life.

Death can be looked upon as the final stage of growth. But only when we have the courage to face the fact of death and our own fear of dying can we know how to live. In other words, we cannot accept our dying if we have not accepted our living. To come to terms with the one is to come to terms with the other. As long as we wish to keep a tight control over both life and death, we will know only frustration, anger, and fear.

In the past the Christian understanding of new life after death made it possible for people to face death defiantly because we saw the possibility of overcoming the ultimate power of death to destroy. However, in our culture today, where Christianity is just one religious view among many, the possibility of resurrection and eternal life may not be the prevalent view. In fact, there are three prominent views regarding death in our society today.

• Death as Extinction. At the point of death, life ceases to exist. There is no afterlife. Death is the end.

• Death as Reincarnation. At death, the soul is reincarnated into another living body on earth. After death, any one of us may become an insect, a cow, a pauper, or a prince. Our behavior in this life destines our body in the next.

• Death as Resurrection. There is a self-conscious existence beyond this life. The essence of one's personhood lives on after death in a new dimension of reality: heaven. Tradition holds that we who believe will share eternally the bliss of fellowship with God in heaven, while those who refuse God's love are eternally separated from God: hell. Although life after death is not a central consideration in the Old Testament, after the resurrection of Jesus it became a central doctrine in the Christian faith. But the development in our belief about life after death has taken centuries. Early Christians looked forward to the immediate return of Christ. They believed that Jesus would soon return to raise the living and the dead. Later, both the apostle Paul and most Christian thinking through the nineteenth century believed that the dead are asleep and at the end of time (general resurrection) will be raised up (1 Corinthians 15:51-55). Today, many Christians believe that life continues immediately after death without any "sleep of the soul." Jesus said to the thief on the cross, "Today you will be with me in Paradise" (Luke 23:43), and we believe that the soul is "lifted up" into heaven at the time of one's death.

As Christians, most of us share in a deep and profound belief that there is a positive, benevolent life after death. This life after death is the promise of Christ to believers and the primary source of comfort for many Christians in times of loss. Since none of us can be totally in control of our own lives, we must trust in God's care. Perhaps our anxiety has less to do with being afraid of death than with pain and suffering and helplessness associated with dying. If we drive fear and depression from one another in Christian love and if we attend to one another well in life's extremes, we will be able to accept death as a transition and a doorway to eternal life.

DISCUSSION STARTERS

Which view best describes your view of what happens after someone dies?
1. Death as Extinction: There is no life after death.
2. Reincarnation: After dying, a person returns to earth as a new person (or animal).
3. Deep Sleep: Those who die go into a state of being like a deep sleep. On the day of judgement it will be decided whether they go to heaven or hell.
4. Immediate Resurrection: Those who believe in Jesus Christ will immediately go to heaven. Those who don't will go to hell.
5. Everlasting Life: Everyone who dies goes to be with God. There is no heaven or hell.
6. Other: _____

BIBLICAL REFLECTIONS (ACTS 7:54-60; REVELATION 7:15-17)

Stephen was the first Christian martyr. He was also one of the first leaders who was not one of the twelve original disciples. In Acts 6:8 it says, "Stephen, full of grace and power, did great wonders and signs among the people." He became such a powerful defender of Christianity that he was arrested by the high priest for blasphemy. Saul would later become Paul, one of the key leaders of the Christian movement.
1. What does Stephen's witness say about life after death?
2. What do Stephen's last words about forgiveness say to you?
3. What do you think happened to Stephen after he died?
4. What does Revelation 7:15-17 say to you about eternal life?
5. How does your understanding of eternal life affect how you live today?

MAKING IT PERSONAL

1. What do you believe happens after someone dies?
2. Have you experienced the death of a loved one? What process did you go through to help you get through the grief? Are there things that still hold you back?
3. How does your faith enable you to face your own mortality?
4. What steps have you taken to prepare for death or for a long-term illness?

_____ Prepared a Will

_____ Prepared a Living Will

_____ Prepared a Durable Power of Attorney

_____ Reviewed Your Life Insurance Policy

_____ Reviewed Your Medical Insurance Benefits

_____ Bought Long-Term Care Insurance

_____ Others:_____

5. How have you shared these thoughts with the people closest to you?

10

Giving Back

SESSION OUTLINE

Getting Started (10 minutes)
- Open with prayer.
- Ask participants to read or review Chapter 10.
- Ask participants to identify the key issues from the reading.

Discussion Starters (15 minutes)
- Use the discussion starters to help participants review the changes they have experienced as they have moved through adulthood.

Biblical Reflections (15 minutes)
- Ask for a volunteer to read aloud Ecclesiastes 2:1-11.
- Divide into small groups of three to four if the group is large.
- Read the "Biblical Reflections" and discuss the questions.

Making It Personal (15 minutes)
- Ask participants to read "Making It Personal."
- Discuss how participants are using the three described strategies. Ask for other suggestions on how to move into the future as adults who are "giving back."

Closing (5 minutes)
- Ask participants to reflect on what they have learned over the last ten sessions—what went well, what could have been improved.
- Close with prayer.

Our generation has always wanted to make a difference in the world. During our formative years, midlife adults experienced a unique slice of American history: the civil rights movement, President Kennedy's assassination, the Vietnam War and the turbulent period of student protests against the war, the assassination of the Rev. Dr. Martin Luther King, Jr., the Nixon years and the Watergate break-in, the post-Watergate malaise, the feminist movement, and the oil embargo. We followed the beat of rock-and-roll, participated in the sexual revolution, and watched astronauts walk on the moon. We were optimistic, hopeful, and out to change the world.

The simple sense that we have "made a difference" in at least some aspect of our lives becomes important to us as we reflect on our life goals and past achievements during midlife. This may be in our role as spouses or parents, some community or church involvement, or an organization or business enterprise. We want to know that our lives do make a difference. Through this midlife reflection, we may also come to the realization that there is more we wish to do.

According to Erik Erikson's theory of psychosocial development, the focal challenge of adulthood is centered around the issue of "generativity" versus stagnation. For many people, this conflict is resolved through the creation and care of children. However, in Erikson's theory, *generativity* is broadly defined and refers not only to the creation and caring of children but also to the production of things and ideas through work. Thus childless couples and single people may guide and care for the next generation by working with other people's children or by helping to create a better world for them (*Childhood and Society*, 2nd edition, by Erik Erikson; Norton, 1963).

True generativity is rooted in our involvement in the larger society, not merely in our own personal sphere of influence. When our desire to make a difference in our world comes from the inside out and is not relied on for identity, power, and wealth but rather is characterized by traits such as authenticity, self-authority, and personal passion, it is more significant. Many of us at midlife have found that our real work, the work that comes from our souls, is participation in the creation of a more humane and just world. In fact, when work is viewed as a mission or passion, people often sense a resurgence of energy.

Some of us in midlife seem unable to care deeply for anything beyond ourselves. We have lost any concern we might have had for other people, especially the younger generation. We are bitter, frustrated, and cynical. We believe life has dealt us one bad blow after another.

When generativity is lacking, the result is a psychological and spiritual stagnation. We feel that life is drab and empty, that we are merely marking time and getting older without fulfilling life expectations. As a result, we are not using our God-given abilities and gifts to make life interesting and zestful. Rather, we become apathetic and resentful, believing life is dull and monotonous.

Why do some of us stagnate while others regenerate and reinvent ourselves at midlife? Perhaps the key to generativity is not so much our activities themselves as it is our attitude toward the activities. Do they lead us to fulfill our values? Are we concerned with those things about which we truly care? As participants in the "me generation," we sometimes become too exclusively involved in ourselves and our own success and neglect the responsibility of caring for others.

Midlife is a time of change and challenge. We are the busiest and the most productive we have ever been and are often at the peak of our earning power. Now that our children are becoming more independent or grown, we are willing to expend more time and energy on our own work and major goals. We have nurtured our children, lost parents, and become grandparents. Even our inevitable encounters with failure and life uncertainty have provided fuel for an incredibly uplifting and powerful period of growth in our lives.

Faith is one of the keys to whether we view midlife from a perspective of generativity or stagnation. Faith requires action. Faith without action is just wishful thinking. Action without faith is just passing time. But faith with action can change the world. That's what we are all called to do—each of us: to grow in faith in our middle-age years and to help others in their journeys of faith.

As we move through the midlife years, we try to reinvent ourselves so that we are able to make a difference, to give something of ourselves back to the world. We learn to cope with our losses and to find new ways for using our gifts. We seek new ways to be married or to be single. We discover new ways to be with our children, grandchildren, or friends. We give ourselves permission to live and do as we see fit, not as others define what is right for us. We deepen our relationship to God and grow in grace. At midlife, we are challenged to reexamine, redefine, renew, and reinvent ourselves. What we will be has not yet come to fruition, but with God's help, we will make a difference.

DISCUSSION STARTERS

Throughout this study you have met a number of people from the Bible who have faced change. Some of these include:
- Abram and Sarai called to leave their homeland
- Mary receiving a message from the angel

- Elizabeth surprised to be having a child in midlife
- Jesus moving from the role of carpenter to the role of Messiah
- Mary dealing with her adult son Jesus
- Mary praying after her son has died
- Naomi and Ruth making decisions after the deaths of their loved ones
- Nicodemus changing his ideas and beliefs about God
- Stephen forgiving his enemies even as he dies

1. Which person best represents the changes you are now facing?
2. Which one challenges you the most?
3. Which one gives you the most hope for the future?

Biblical Reflections (Ecclesiastes 2:1-11)

In this passage we see the author of Ecclesiastes reviewing his life and asking the question that many of us ask as we move through middle adulthood: "Is this all there is?" As the writer reviewed his life he realized that although he had amassed large amounts of property and wealth and had indulged in all sorts of things designed to bring pleasure, "all was vanity and a chasing after wind."

1. In what ways do you relate to the experiences of the writer of this passage?
2. What advice would you give to a friend who was expressing the feelings found in this passage?

Making It Personal

As you plan for the future consider these three strategies:

1. Be ready to make difficult choices.

Which values are still important? Do we really need that big house that we dreamed about when we were first married? Do I really need to spend so much time perfecting my golf game? Can I lead a fulfilling life with a spouse or children? How can I make a difference in my work, church, or community?

2. Remain open to change.

We can't keep adding new projects, new responsibilities, or new values without getting rid of some old ones. Each stage of life calls for the substitution of new skills, activities, and relationships for old ones that are no longer important in our lives. What is God calling us to be? What is most important in our lives at this time? What do I need to stop doing in order to make a difference in the world today?

3. Be open to new roles and responsibilities.

We assume the roles of teachers or mentors—encouragers and supporters of others. We are no longer interested in just attending meetings and generating ideas; we also want to see our ideas carried out. We know that if we want to make a difference in the world, we must stop dreaming about it and get started.